GCSE
Mathematics
FOR SCIENTISTS

Bob McDuell

Every effort has been made to trace copyright holders and to obtain permission for the use of copyright material. The authors and publishers will gladly receive information enabling them to rectify any error or omission in subsequent editions.

First published 1998

Letts Educational
Schools and Colleges Division
9–15 Aldine Street
London W12 8AW
Tel. 0181 740 2270
Fax 0181 740 2280

Text © Bob McDuell 1998

Editorial, design and production by Moondisks Ltd, Cambridge

All our rights reserved. No part of this publication may be reproduced, stored in a retrieval system, or transmitted, in any form or by any means, electronic, mechanical, photocopying, recording or otherwise, without prior permission of Letts Educational.

British Library Cataloguing-in-Publication Data
A CIP record for this book is available from the British Library.

ISBN 1 84085 150 3

Printed and bound in Great Britain

Letts Educational is the trading name of BPP (Letts Educational) Ltd.

Contents

	page
Introduction	4
1 Using a calculator	5
2 Using formulae	15
3 Measuring length, mass and time	21
4 Handling data	30
Answers	42

Introduction

This Letts *GCSE Mathematics for Scientists* has been specially written for all of the new GCSE syllabuses and is suitable for both Foundation and Higher tiers. It is closely linked to the National Curriculum and will help you master the key mathematical concepts in key stage 4 Science.

The book is divided into four sections: Using a calculator; Using formulae; Measuring length, mass and time; Handling data. Each section gives explanations, examples and practice questions which will help you develop the key mathematical skills necessary for GCSE Double or Single Award Science.

We hope that this book will help you to progress in GCSE Science courses.

Key

 Example

 Question

1 Using a calculator

You can use a calculator in any Science examination. The calculator you use must not be a graphical or programmable calculator, which might be used illegally in an examination to recall information.

What type of calculator should you use? This is not a straightforward question to answer. You should use a calculator you can use correctly. An expensive scientific calculator may lead to errors when you use it. For example, if you divide 1 by 9999, the reading on the scientific calculator will be 1.00010001E−4. Students often write this as the answer. The correct answer, to four significant figures, is

1.000×10^{-4} or 0.0001.

A cheap four-function calculator bought for £1.99 would enable you to add, subtract, multiply and divide and use limited memory functions. For the calculation above, it would give you the answer 0.000 100 0. You would still have to correct the answer to the correct number of significant figures.

Make sure your calculator is working correctly. Remember, it must be battery-powered rather than mains-powered. Always have a spare set of batteries with you just in case.

When setting papers, examiners try to set questions that would not seriously disadvantage a candidate without a calculator. Usually the figures work out easily, especially at Foundation level.

Let us look at an example.

> **Ex 1.1** A current of 4 A is passed through copper(II) sulphate solution for 2 hours. Calculate the mass of copper deposited.

You need a value for the Faraday constant. Some Examination Boards give a value of 96 000 C and some give a value of 96 500 C. The former value simplifies the arithmetic but the second value is more accurate.

Using 1 faraday = 96 000 C

$$\text{Quantity of electricity passed} = 4 \times 2 \times 60 \times 60 \text{ C}$$

$$= \frac{4 \times 2 \times 60 \times 60}{96\,000} \text{ F}$$

$$= 0.3 \text{ F}$$

The formula mass of copper (64 g) is produced by 2 F. (This is because copper ions have a 2+ charge and 2 moles of electrons or 2 faradays are required to deposit 64 g of copper.)

$$\text{Mass of copper deposited by } 0.3\,F = \frac{64 \times 0.3}{2}\,g$$

$$= 9.6\,g$$

Using 1 faraday = 96 500 C.

$$\text{Quantity of electricity passed} = 4 \times 2 \times 60 \times 60\,C$$

$$= \frac{4 \times 2 \times 60 \times 60}{96\,000}\,F$$

$$= 0.298\,F$$

The formula mass of copper (64 g) is produced by 2 F.

$$\text{Mass of copper deposited by } 0.3\,F = \frac{64 \times 0.298}{2}\,g$$

$$= 9.54\,g$$

In both cases all of the steps of the calculation are shown. If you only write down the answer 9.6 g or 9.54 g, the examiner will not be able to follow the steps of your calculation. If you made any mistake in the calculation, the examiner could not give you any credit for correct things you have done.

It is essential that you show, on paper, all of the steps of the calculation so the examiner can give you the maximum number of marks.

The answer shown on the calculator is actually 9.536 g. It is usual to correct the answer to **3 significant figures**. This means three figures that have meaning – in this case 9 units, 5 tenths and 4 hundredths. Notice how we have corrected the answer by rounding up the 6 in the third place of decimals. If there is 0 to 4 in the third place of decimals, it is ignored. If there is 5 to 9, the number in the second place of decimals is rounded up. For example, 1.123 becomes 1.12 and 1.236 becomes 1.24.

> **Q 1.1** Correct the following to 3 significant figures
>
> a 10.32 _____ b 100.9 _____
>
> c 23.48 _____ d 24.128 _____
>
> e 12.009 _____

1 Using a calculator

Students using a calculator often make silly mistakes. They assume the answer on the calculator will always be correct.

Ex 1.2 Multiply 2.1 by 22.9.

Without using a calculator you should realise the answer will be about 46. This is because 2.1 is just greater than 2 and 22.9 is just less than 23. The result of $2 \times 23 = 46$.

Q 1.2 Without using a calculator, choose the answer closest to the correct answer from the four given.

    a 100×99
       i 100   **ii** 1000   **iii** 10 000   **iv** 100 000

    b 2.9×21.1
       i 45   **ii** 62   **iii** 8   **iv** 142

    c 0.099×45.2
       i 0.45   **ii** 4.5   **iii** 45   **iv** 450

    d 0.099×0.099
       i 0.1   **ii** 0.01   **iii** 0.001   **iv** 0.0001

Number

Most of the calculations on GCSE papers involve the accurate use of one or more of the four operations: addition, subtraction, multiplication and division. The following examples will check that you can do these four operations correctly. You can use a calculator.

Q 1.3 a i $37 + 46 + 83 + 129 =$ _____
      ii $139 + 1.47 + 21.38 =$ _____
      iii $398 + 103 =$ _____
      iv $435.7 + 13.96 + 0.177 =$ _____
      v $1390 + 236 + 36.45 =$ _____

b i What is the difference between 273 and 350? _____
  ii 234.5 − 117.3 = _____
  iii 23.7 − 13.49 = _____
  iv 211.11 − 98.4 = _____
  v 239.0 − 23.73 = _____

c i 13 × 17 = _____
  ii 13.9 × 4.3 = _____
  iii 23.56 × 0.8 = _____
  iv 0.75 × 0.09 = _____
  v 295 × 345 = _____

d i 96 ÷ 12 = _____
  ii 46 ÷ 5 = _____
  iii 23.7 ÷ 4.2 = _____
  iv 123 ÷ 11 = _____
  v 139.65 ÷ 29 = _____

If you find you have made mistakes try some more similar examples. Remember, every time you make an arithmetical mistake you are likely to lose at least one mark. If you do this several times it could affect your final grade.

Squares and square roots

The square of a number is the result of multiplying the number by itself. For example, two squared (written as 2^2) is $2 \times 2 = 4$.

You may have a squared button on your calculator. If you have, you enter the number and press this button and it will give the squared number. For example, to find out the square of 9, you do the following:

  enter 9   press x^2 answer 81

Now try the following examples.

1 Using a calculator

Q 1.4 **a** $11^2 = $ _____ **b** $100^2 = $ _____
      c $13.2^2 = $ _____ **d** $0.12^2 = $ _____
      e $1.02^2 = $ _____

The area of a square with side 5 cm, is obtained by multiplying 5 by 5, i.e. 5^2. The answer is 25 cm². The **square root** of 25 is the number which, when multiplied by itself, gives 25. The square root of 25 is 5.

The sign for square root is $\sqrt{}$.

This table shows the square roots of some numbers you should know.

number	1	4	9	16	25	36	49	64	81	100	121	144	169	225	400	625
square root	1	2	3	4	5	6	7	8	9	10	11	12	13	15	20	25

If you want the square root of 50, you should realise that it will be very slightly greater than 7.

You can use your calculator to work out square roots using the square root button. Enter the number. Then press $\sqrt{}$. The answer is shown on the display. For example, if you want to find out the square root of 50, you do the following:

    enter 50   press $\sqrt{}$ answer 7.071

Q 1.5 **a** **Without using a calculator**, write down the square roots of the following numbers, to the nearest whole number. For example, $\sqrt{50} = 7$.
      i $\sqrt{120} = $ _____ **ii** $\sqrt{78} = $ _____
      iii $\sqrt{40} = $ _____ **iv** $\sqrt{150} = $ _____
      v $\sqrt{90000} = $ _____ (Hint: $90\,000 = 400 \times 225$)
      b Use the calculator to work out the following.
      i $\sqrt{200} = $ _____ **ii** $\sqrt{456} = $ _____
      iii $\sqrt{23.4} = $ _____ **iv** $\sqrt{3.46} = $ _____
      v $\sqrt{0.006} = $ _____

Fractions

There are different types of fraction. These include **vulgar fractions** (sometimes just called **fractions**) and **decimal fractions** (sometimes just called **decimals**).

Vulgar fractions

A vulgar fraction consists of two parts: a **numerator** and a **denominator**. The number at the top is the numerator and the number at the bottom is the denominator. For example, in the fraction two-thirds, written as $\frac{2}{3}$, the numerator is 2 and the denominator is 3.

> **Q 1.6** What are the numerator and the denominator in the fraction three-quarters?

Imagine a cake cut into three equal pieces. The fraction two-thirds consists of two of these three pieces as shown in this diagram.

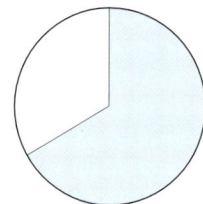

> **Q 1.7** Shade three-eighths of this rectangle.
>
> What fraction remains unshaded?
>
> _____
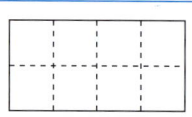

What is special about the three fractions below?

$$\frac{2}{3} \quad \frac{4}{6} \quad \frac{10}{15}$$

They all have the same value. They are called **equivalent fractions**. If you divide the numerator and the denominator in four-sixths by 2, the answer is two-thirds. If you divide the numerator and the denominator in ten-fifteenths by 5, the answer is again two-thirds.

1 Using a calculator

 1.8 a Put a ring around fractions in the list that are equivalent fractions to one-half.

$$\frac{20}{40} \quad \frac{36}{65} \quad \frac{14}{30} \quad \frac{24}{48} \quad \frac{18}{30}$$

b Complete the following equivalent fractions to three-fifths.

$$\frac{9}{} \quad \frac{15}{} \quad \frac{}{10} \quad \frac{}{20}$$

Decimal fractions

The decimal fraction 0.25 (we say 'nought point two five') can be written

units	tenths	hundredths	thousandths
0	2	5	0

It represents two tenths and five hundredths, or twenty-five hundredths.

 1.9 In a similar way represent:

a 0.4 _____

b 0.12 _____

c 0.375 _____

d 1.205 _____

e 6.007 _____

Converting fractions to decimals

The fraction three-fifths can be represented by $\frac{3}{5}$. To convert this to a decimal, the numerator is divided by the denominator (3 ÷ 5). When you work this out it gives an answer of 0.6. (A common mistake is to divide the larger number by the smaller number and get 1.66.)

Converting decimals to fractions

To convert 0.65 to a fraction, write it as 65 hundredths, i.e. $\frac{65}{100}$. Then reduce it to the simplest fraction by dividing the numerator and the denominator by five. This will give you $\frac{13}{20}$.

GCSE Mathematics for Scientists

Q 1.10 a Convert the following fractions to decimals.

    i $\frac{1}{4}$ _____   **ii** $\frac{1}{3}$ _____

    iii $\frac{7}{8}$ _____   **iv** $\frac{6}{10}$ _____

    v $\frac{4}{11}$ _____

b Convert the following decimals into simplest fractions.

    i 0.75 _____   **ii** 0.45 _____

    iii 0.675 _____   **iv** 0.95 _____

    v 0.24 _____

Percentages

Percentages are another way of expressing a fraction. A percentage is a fraction of 100.

Turning a fraction into a percentage

Multiply the fraction by 100, for example

$$\frac{1}{4} \times 100 = 25\%$$

Turning a percentage into a fraction

Divide the percentage by 100, for example

$$30\% = \frac{30}{100} = \frac{3}{10}$$

Remember that if you add up percentages, the sum total will always be 100%.

1 Using a calculator

Q 1.11 a Convert the following fractions into percentages. Give your answers to 3 significant figures.

  i $\frac{1}{2}$ _____   ii $\frac{3}{4}$ _____

  iii $\frac{5}{8}$ _____   iv $\frac{6}{11}$ _____

  v $\frac{37}{40}$ _____

b Convert the following percentages into the simplest fractions

  i 80% _____   ii 12% _____

  iii 45% _____   iv 93% _____

  v 65% _____

c A compound contains 52.2 % carbon and 13.0% hydrogen. The only other element present is oxygen. What is the percentage of oxygen?

_____

Proportion

Here are some results of an experiment where the force is increased on a stretched metal wire. Each time the extension is measured.

force in N	10	20	30	40	50	60	70	80
extension in mm	1.5	3.0	4.5	6.0	7.5	9.0	10.5	12.0

— input better
outcome side

Look at these results. You might conclude that as the force increases the extension increases. This is a low level answer.

Looking at the results you might notice that the extension increases by 1.5 mm for each 100 N increase in force. This is a better answer.

The best answer is that the extension is **directly proportional** to the force. As the force increases the extension increases regularly. The graph goes through the origin, i.e. (0,0).

On page 35 you will find a grid for plotting these results and drawing a straight line.

Here are some results of another experiment where some gas is trapped and the pressure applied to the gas is changed. Each time the pressure is changed the volume is recorded. All results are taken at the same temperature.

pressure in kPa	100	140	195	275	330	500
volume in cm³	25	18	13	9	7.5	5

The first thing you should notice is that as the pressure increases, the volume decreases.

Now try multiplying pressure and volume together in each case.

$P \times V$	2500	2520	2535	2475	2475	2500

You will notice that $P \times V$ is almost the same in each case. It is not exactly the same because of experimental error taking the readings. For example, a difference of $0.5 cm^3$ in measuring the volume in the third result alters $P \times V$ by almost 100.

We can write down that $P \times V$ is a constant. As the pressure increases the volume decreases. The volume of the gas is said to be **inversely proportional** to the pressure.

On page 36 you will plot these results. A graph of P against V is a curve. A graph of P against $\frac{1}{V}$ gives a straight line which passes through (0,0).

2 Using formulae

There are a number of formulae you must remember for your GCSE examination. There are others you can be given and might then be expected to use.

Formulae you must remember
Foundation tier papers

$V = IR$ voltage = current × resistance
(volt, V) (ampere, A) (ohm, Ω)

$P = VI$ power = voltage × current
(watt, W) (volt, V) (ampere, A)

$v = \dfrac{d}{t}$ average speed = distance travelled ÷ time
(metre/second, m/s) (metre, m) (second, s)

$a = \dfrac{v_2 - v_1}{t}$ acceleration = increase in velocity ÷ time
(metre/second squared, m/s²) (metre/second, m/s) (second, s)

(NB Candidates frequently give the unit of acceleration as metre/second/second, m/s/s. This is incorrect.)

$p = \dfrac{F}{A}$ pressure = force ÷ area
(pascal, Pa) (newton, N) (metre squared, m²)

(NB The unit pascal is equivalent to 1 newton/metre squared, 1 N/m².)

$W = Fd$ work done in the direction of the force = energy transferred = force × distance moved in the direction of the force

(joule, J) (newton, N) (metre, m)

$E = Pt$ energy transferred = power × time
(joule, J) (watt, W) (second, s)

GCSE Mathematics for Scientists

Higher tier papers

For Higher tier the formulae on page 15 should be known and, in addition, the ones below.

$F = ma$	force (newton, N)	= mass (kilogram, kg)	×	acceleration (metres per second squared, m/s²)
$I = \dfrac{Q}{t}$	current (ampere, A)	= charge flow (coulomb, C)	÷	time (second, s)
$v = f\lambda$	wave speed (metre/second, m/s)	= frequency (hertz, Hz)	×	wavelength (metre, m)

You should check the syllabus at this point as the requirements for individual syllabuses vary.

Example of the use of these formulae

An object travels 10 000 metres in 1 minute. What is the average speed?

The formula you need to use is

$$v = \frac{d}{t}$$

The distance is 10 000 metres but the time must be converted into seconds: 1 minute is 60 seconds.

$$\text{Average speed} = 10\,000 \div 60 = 166.7 \text{ m/s}$$

There are three stages in doing this.

1 Write down the formula.

2 Substitute the numbers in this formula

3 Write down the answer, with the correct unit.

It is important that you follow all three stages to make sure you score all the marks. Also, if you make an error, you could still be given marks for some part of the calculation.

Here is an example for you to try:

> **Q 2.1** A force of 100 N acts on an area of 20 cm². Calculate the pressure.

2 Using formulae

Other formulae
There are other formulae that you do not have to remember but that may be given to you to use on the examination paper.

$E = Pt$ energy transferred = power × time
            (kilowatt hour, kWh) = (kilowatt, kW)   (hour, h)

$P = \dfrac{W}{t}$ power = work done ÷ time taken
            (watt, W)   (joule, J)   (second, s)

            weight = mass × gravitational field strength
            (newton, N)   (kilogram, kg)   (newton/kilogram, N/kg)

Transformation of a formula
Sometimes you have to change the subject of a formula before you can use it in a calculation. This is usually only on Higher tier papers.

For example, if a vehicle is moving at 50 m/s for 30 s, what distance does it cover? You are expected to use the formula:

$$v = \dfrac{d}{t}$$

There are three ways of doing this. Any of these would be acceptable.

1 Substitute the numbers in the equation and then re-arrange it:

$$50 = \dfrac{d}{30}$$

Multiply both sides by 30

$d = 30 \times 50 = 1500 \, \text{m}$

2 Rearrange the formula first and then substitute. Multiply both sides of the equation by t:

$d = vt$
$d = 30 \times 50 = 1500 \, \text{m}$

3 Represent the relationship by a triangle:

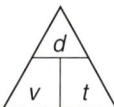

If you cover up v with your finger, what is left is the rest of the equation to find v.

$$v = \dfrac{d}{t}$$

If you now cover d with your finger, you can write $d = vt$

Finally, if you cover t, you can write $t = \dfrac{d}{v}$

Having got the relationship you require you can then proceed as in **1**.

Here are some for you to try. Use all three methods for the first one. You can then decide which one you are happy with and use it in the others.

> **Q 2.2 a** Calculate the distance moved by a force of 10 N which does 50 J of work.
>
> **b** A wave has a speed of 1500 m/s and a frequency of 250 Hz. Calculate the wavelength.
>
> **c** Air pushes on a window with a pressure of 100 000 Pa. What is the force acting on a window with an area of 6 m²?

Using two relationships together

Sometimes, at Higher tier, you have to use two relationships together as in the following example.

> **Ex 2.1** A 12 V car headlamp bulb has a resistance of 4 W. Calculate the power rating of the bulb.

You need to use two equations:

$V = IR$ voltage = current × resistance
$P = VI$ power = voltage × current

You could write the first equation as

$$I = \dfrac{V}{R}$$

substitute for I in the second equation,

$$P = \dfrac{V^2}{R}$$

and then substitute in this equation $V = 12$ and $R = 4$:

$P = 12 \times 12 \div 4$
$ = 36\,W$

2 Using formulae

Alternatively, you could do the calculation in two stages. Use $V = IR$ to calculate the current:

$I = \frac{V}{R}$
$= 12 \div 4$
$= 3\,\text{A}.$

Then use $P = VI$ to calculate the power:

$P = 12 \times 3 = 36\,\text{W}$

It is probably easier to use the second method, but try the following calculations by both methods.

> **Q 2.3 a** A hydraulic ramp in a garage lifts a car of mass 800 kg to a height of 1.8 m.
> Show that the work done doing this is 14 440 J.
> Use $g = 10\,\text{N/kg}$.
>
> **b** The ramp lifts at a steady speed of 0.2 m/s to a height of 1.8 m. Calculate the useful power output of the ramp in lifting the car.

Although most calculations involving algebraic equations occur in Sc4 (Physics), they also appear in other branches of science.

These are examples of calculations in Sc3 (Chemistry)

> **Q 2.4** $n = \frac{m}{M}$
>
> where n is number of moles, m is the mass in g, and M is the mass of 1 mole (formula mass) in g.
>
> Show this relationship in a triangle:
>
>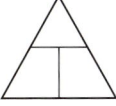

> **Ex 2.2** Calculate the number of moles of potassium (K) in 78 g of potassium. (Relative atomic mass of potassium, K = 39.)
>
> $m = 78\,\text{g}, \qquad M = 39\,\text{g}$
>
> Number of moles of potassium, $n = 78 \div 39 = 2$

Q 2.5 Here are some for you to try.
(Relative atomic masses, K = 39, O = 16, H = 1.)

a Calculate the number of moles (formula masses) of potassium oxide, K_2O in 9.4 g.

b Calculate the mass in g of 0.2 moles of potassium hydroxide, KOH.

c Calculate the mass in g of 0.5 moles of water, H_2O.

d 0.1 moles of potassium hydroxide is dissolved in 100 g of water. What mass of potassium hydroxide is needed to make up 1 dm^3 of potassium hydroxide solution of the same concentration? (Ignore any change in volume when potassium hydroxide is dissolved in water.)

3 Measuring length, mass and time

In practical work many of your measurements will be of length, mass and time. You will be expected to make your measurements as accurately as you can with the apparatus you have to use.

Measurements of length

Measurements of length are usually made with some kind of ruler or tape. Very short distances may be measured in millimetres (mm). Longer distances, over about 5 cm (for instance the dimensions of a page of this book), are best measured in centimetres (cm). Much longer distances, such as the length of a football pitch, are best measured in metres (m).

> **Q 3.1** What metric unit can be used to measure longer distances, e.g. between two towns?
>
> _____

Remember there are 10 mm in each centimetre and 1000 mm in each metre.

A length of 155 mm can be written as 15.5 cm or 0.115 m.

> **Q 3.2 a** Write each of the following distances in centimetres.
>
>   **i** 274 mm _____
>
>   **ii** 9 mm _____
>
>   **iii** 1320 mm _____
>
> **b** Write each of the following distances in millimetres.
>
>   **i** 149 cm _____
>
>   **ii** 1.45 m _____
>
>   **iii** 12.7 cm _____

c This diagram shows a ruler alongside a piece of metal.

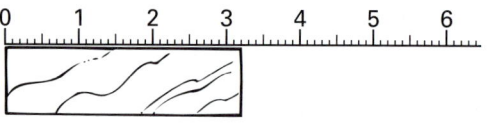

What is the length of the piece of metal in **i** mm and **ii** cm?

i _____ mm   **ii** _____ cm

d Write down the lengths of these lines in mm and in cm

i ──────────────────────   _____ mm

_____ cm

ii ──────────────────   _____ mm

_____ cm

iii ────────────────────────   _____ mm

_____ cm

Sometimes you will be expected to make a measurement a number of times and calculate an average. It is not necessary to repeat any measurement above because they do not change and you would get the same measurement each time.

Q 3.3 Which of these measurements should be carried out a number of times and averaged?

a The length of a pendulum.

b The distance travelled by a model car when it runs off a slope.

c The length of magnesium ribbon used in an experiment.

d The length of a growing leaf over a period of months.

e The length of a baby over the first six months of life.

3 Measuring length, mass and time

Measurements of mass
Measurements of mass are called weighings. Weighings are made on some type of **balance**. The units used when carrying out weighings in the laboratory are grams (g).

$$1\,g = 1000 \text{ milligrams (mg)}$$
$$1000\,g = 1 \text{ kilogram (kg)}$$
$$1000\,kg = 1 \text{ tonne}$$

Measurements of time
Time in experiments is usually measured in units of seconds (s) and minutes (min). Longer times are measured in hours or days. It is important to remember that there are 60 seconds in each minute and 60 minutes in each hour.

Often students write one minute and thirty seconds as 1.30 minutes. Remember, thirty seconds is half a minute and the time should be written as 1.50 minutes.

It is often safer to record your times in seconds, provided this does not give such a large number.

For instance, 2 minutes and 15 seconds = 135 s.

Remember that 0.1 minutes is 6 seconds.

Q 3.4 a Write these times in seconds.

　　i 1 minute and 45 seconds _____

　　ii 3 minutes and 7 seconds _____

　　iii 5 minutes and 23 seconds _____

b Write these times in minutes and seconds.

　　i 3.0 minutes _____

　　ii 1.1 minutes _____

　　iii 2.4 minutes _____

Some timing experiments are carried out electronically. For example, timing races in swimming or athletics can be carried out electronically when times to the nearest 0.01 second can be made. However, in the laboratory pupils often use hand-held stopwatches. These record times to the nearest 0.01 second. You cannot completely rely on these times. There is a delay when you stop and start a hand-held stopwatch. You should only use times to the nearest 0.1 second.

GCSE Mathematics for Scientists

Q 3.5 Here are some readings on a hand-held stopwatch. Correct each reading to the nearest 0.1 s.

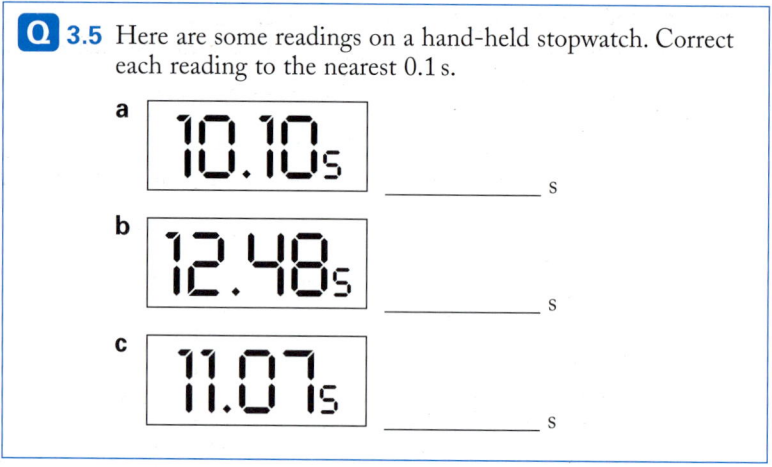

a _____ s

b _____ s

c _____ s

Area

This diagram shows an irregular leaf shape drawn on a piece of squared paper. Each small square has a side of 1 cm. The square has an area of 1 cm².

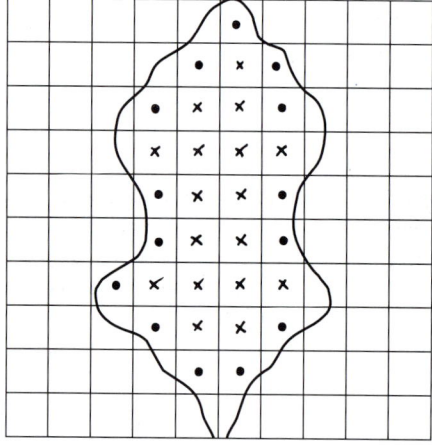

Let us work out the area of the leaf. We count up the number of whole squares covered by the leaf. Then we count up the number of squares more than half-covered by the leaf and finally the number less than half-covered.

Number of whole squares covered by the leaf = 17
Number of squares more than half-covered by the leaf = 14
Number less than half-covered by the leaf = 13

3 Measuring length, mass and time

We now approximate by counting each square more than half-covered as a whole square and we disregard all squares less than half-covered.

In our example the area is 17 + 14 + 0 = 31 cm².

> **Q 3.6** Work out the area of this leaf using the same method.
>
>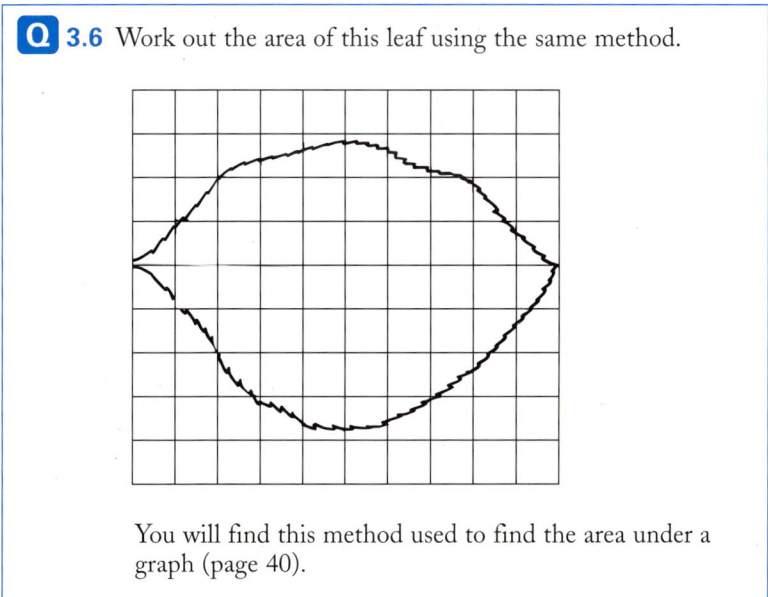
>
> You will find this method used to find the area under a graph (page 40).

Volume

Volume is the space which a substance occupies.

A 250 cm³ measuring cylinder is partly filled with water. An irregularly shaped piece of Plasticine is dropped into the water. The level of the water in the measuring cylinder rises. The volume of the Plasticine can be found by finding the difference in the readings on the measuring cylinder. This is summarised in the diagram below.

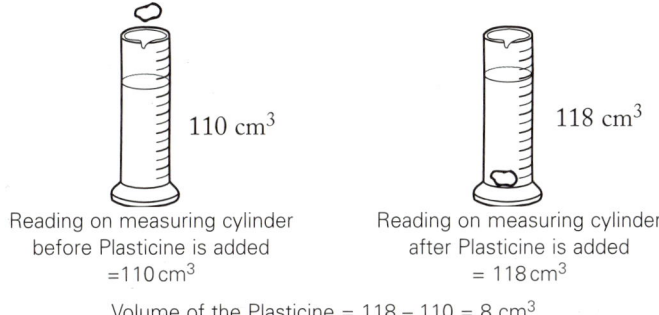

Reading on measuring cylinder before Plasticine is added =110 cm³

Reading on measuring cylinder after Plasticine is added = 118 cm³

Volume of the Plasticine = 118 − 110 = 8 cm³

If the same piece of Plasticine is made into a ball, exactly the same readings are obtained.

Finally, if the same piece of Plasticine is made into a cube 2 cm × 2 cm × 2 cm, again the same difference of 8 cm³ is obtained.

Volume is measured in cubic centimetres (cm³), cubic decimetres (dm³) or cubic metres (m³).

$1\,dm^3 = 1000\,cm^3$

> **Q 3.7** A decimetre is 10 cm. How many cubic decimetres are there in a cubic metre? _____

There are other volume measurements you may see. A cubic decimetre is the same as 1 litre (l). A cubic centimetre is the same as a millilitre (ml).

Use of scale

We often use scale diagrams to represent either very large or very small objects.

This diagram shows the larvae of two insects, the stonefly and the mayfly. These larvae are called nymphs.

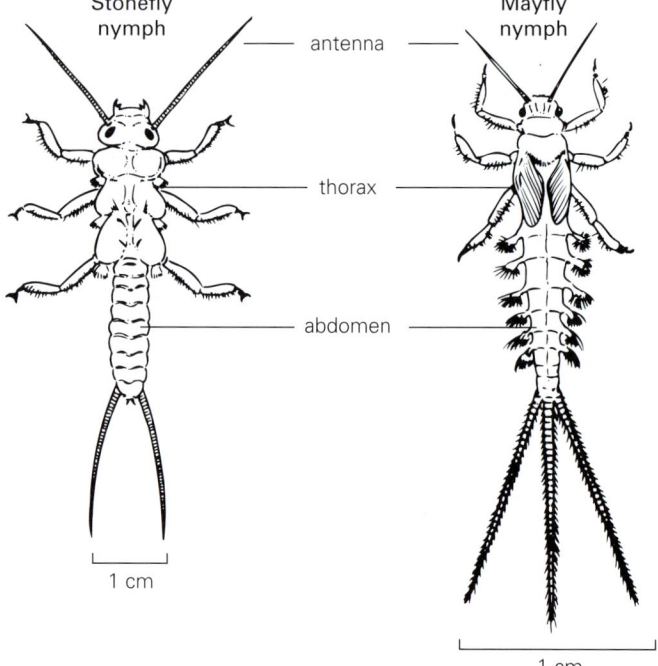

3 Measuring length, mass and time

 3.1 How long is the abdomen of the stonefly nymph?

Measure the length of the abdomen on the diagram. Your measurement should be 1.8 cm. As the diagram is to a scale of 1 : 1 the length of the abdomen is 1.8 cm. If a scale of 2 : 1 had been used (i.e. 1 cm represented by 2 cm on the diagram), the actual length would be

1.8 ÷ 2 = 0.9 cm

> **Q 3.8 a** What is the actual length of the stonefly nymph?
>
> _____
>
> **b** What is the actual length of the mayfly nymph?
>
> _____
>
> The drawing of the mayfly nymph is larger than that of the stonefly nymph.
>
> **c** Why can using different scales for the two be misleading?
>
> _____
>
> _____

Perimeter and area of a rectangle

A rectangle has four sides and four right angles. In this rectangle, AB and CD are equal in length and BC and AD are equal in length.

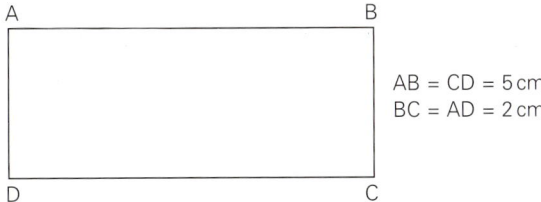

AB = CD = 5 cm
BC = AD = 2 cm

The perimeter of a rectangle is the distance all round it. In this case,

AB + BC + CD + AD = 5 + 2 + 5 + 2 = 14 cm

NB The perimeter is a distance and therefore its units are cm.

GCSE Mathematics for Scientists

Q 3.9 a Work out the perimeter of a rectangle 10 cm × 4 cm

_____

  b A rectangle has a perimeter of 26 cm. The lengths of its sides are whole numbers of cm. Write down the dimensions of possible rectangles.

_____

_____

The area of a rectangle can be found by multiplying the lengths of AB and BC together. In the rectangle ABCD above, the area of the rectangle is $5 \times 2 = 10 \text{ cm}^2$.

Q 3.10 Finish the table showing the lengths and breadths of some rectangles and the areas of these rectangles.

Length in cm	Breadth in cm	Area in cm^2
6	4	
7	5	
12		24
12.3	1.9	
13		93

Volume of a cuboid

Each side of this cuboid is 3 cm long.

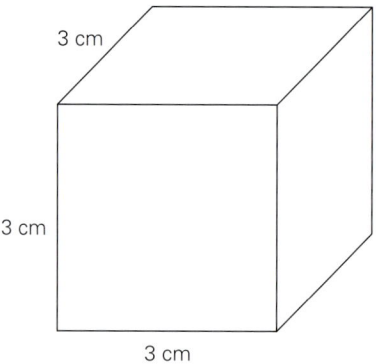

The volume of this cuboid is $3 \times 3 \times 3 = 27 \text{ cm}^3$.

Q 3.11 a What is the volume of a cuboid where each side has a length of 5 cm? _____

b A cuboid has a volume of 1000 cm^3. What is the length of each side? _____

c A carton of fruit juice contains 1 litre of fruit juice. The base of the container is 9.5 cm × 6 cm. What is the minimum height of the container? _____

(Remember: 1 litre = 1000 cm^3.)

4 Handling data

There are many questions on GCSE papers which involve your using data. This may involve putting data into a table, drawing charts or graphs, and using the data to draw conclusions or answer questions.

Tables

Usually data is given to you in the question in the form of a table. You will, however, have to construct tables of data in Sc1 coursework.

Remember to construct the table before you start collecting your results.

Your table must have at least two columns: one for the variable you change (independent variable) and one for the measurements you collect (dependent variable). You may add other columns if you have to process the results.

Here is an example of a table.

concentration of acid in mol/dm^3	time in s	$\frac{1}{t}$ in per s
0.2	300	0.0033 or 33 × 10^{-4}
0.4	250	0.0040 or 40 × 10^{-4}
0.6	185	0.0054 or 54 × 10^{-4}
0.8	155	0.0065 or 65 × 10^{-4}
1.0	120	0.0083 or 83 × 10^{-4}

Do not forget to put in units. Putting units in the heading avoids having to repeat them for each entry.

Notice that the concentrations of acid are arranged in increasing order. Doing this will help you to see any patterns in the results.

4 Handling data

 4.1 This diagram shows the distribution of aphids (greenfly) on two sycamore trees. Part (a) shows the aphids on the leaf in a strong wind. Part (b) shows the aphids after the wind had died down.

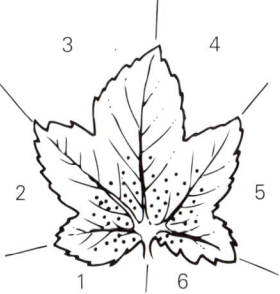

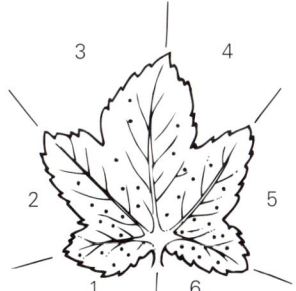

a Distribution of aphids in a strong wind

b Distribution of aphids after wind has died down

Count the number of aphids in each sector in the two drawings.

Record your results in a suitable table.

Pie charts

You might have to construct and use pie charts on Foundation level papers.

This circle is divided up into 20 sectors. Each sector represents 5%. When constructing a pie chart, you should take the largest percentage first. The other percentages must be taken in order.

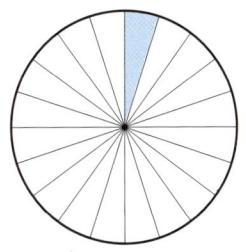

Here is some data. The table shows the world energy sources as percentages. Remember, the percentages must add up to 100%.

energy source	percentage
oil	40
natural gas	20
solid fuel	30
other sources	

GCSE Mathematics for Scientists

Q 4.2
a What is the percentage of 'other sources'?

b Here the oil and natural gas segments have been drawn. Finish this pie chart by adding the other two segments.

Pictograms

This pictogram shows how long reserves of different metal ores should last. Each metal bar represents 10 years.

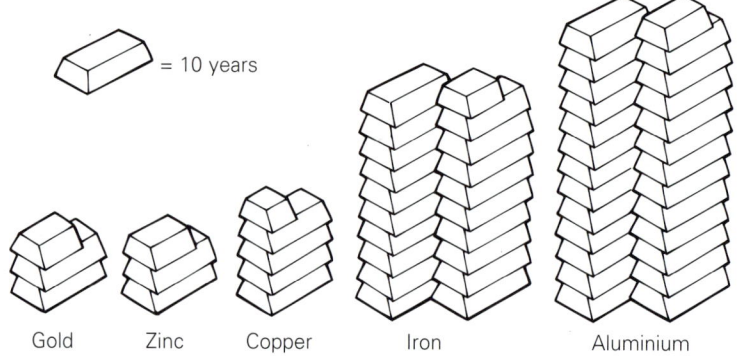

Deposits of gold ores will last about 28 years. There are two metal bars (that is 20 years) and one not complete (estimate 8 years).

Q 4.3 How long will deposits of the other metal ores last?

Zinc _____ years   Copper _____ years

Iron _____ years   Aluminium _____ years.

4 Handling data

Bar charts

Bar charts are frequently used on Foundation level papers.

This table gives the hardness of water in different cities in Great Britain.

city	hardness of water in mg/dm^3
Bath	300
Birmingham	20
Cardiff	30
Leeds	140
Manchester	100
Norwich	320
Nottingham	130
Salisbury	240
Southampton	

These can be shown in a bar chart.

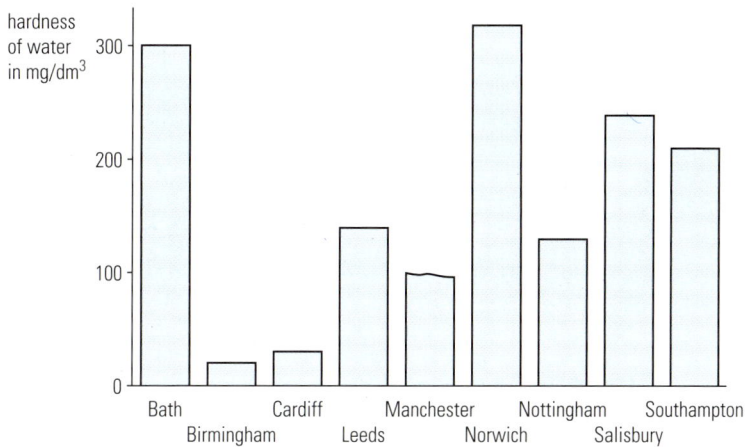

There is no link between the hardness in water in these different cities. It would be incorrect to try to draw a line graph.

> **Q 4.4** What is the hardness in Southampton? _____ mg/dm^3

The examiner will look closely at the top of each bar you draw. There would probably be two marks for drawing this bar chart. The bar for Manchester is not drawn level. The examiner would deduct one mark for each mistake. There would be only one mark for this effort.

GCSE Mathematics for Scientists

Histograms (bar graphs)

Students frequently confuse **histograms** with bar charts. Remember, in the bar chart you have just seen there were no links between the hardness of water in different cities.

The locust is an insect that has an exoskeleton. This does not stretch as the animal grows. It sheds its exoskeleton when it moults and replaces it with a new and larger one. It therefore grows in steps. This histogram shows the length of a locust over about a month. Notice the bars are joined up. There is a relationship between the bars. Each bar is longer than the one before it.

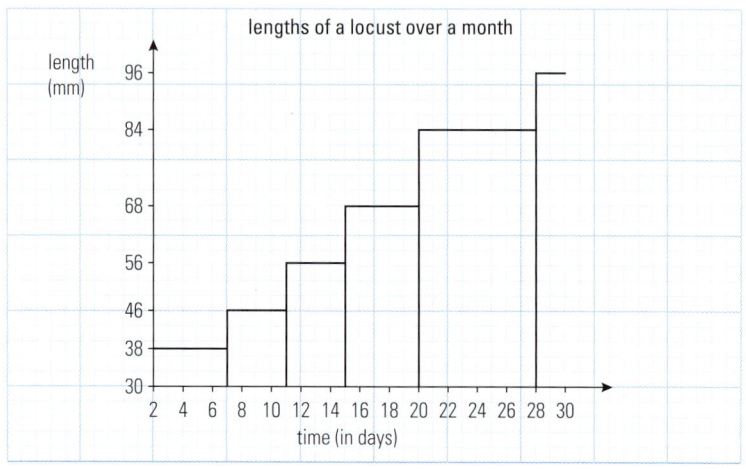

Line graphs

Line graphs are the most frequent way of representing data on GCSE papers. On Foundation level papers you will be given a grid with axes labelled and scales chosen. All of your plots will be easy to make and all of the plots will be on the line you are expected to draw.

On page 13 you saw results for the extension of a metal wire when different forces are applied. Here they are again.

force in N	10	20	30	40	50	60	70	80
extension in mm	1.5	3.0	4.5	6.0	7.5	9.0	10.5	12.0

4 Handling data

Q 4.5 Plot these results on the grid below. The first two have been done for you. Draw a line through all of the plots.

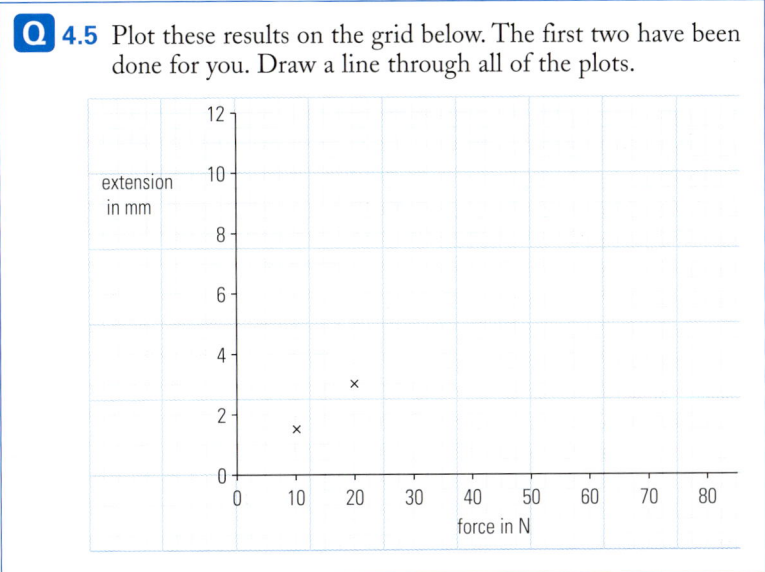

You should have a straight line which goes through all of your plots and through the origin. The straight line tells us that the extension is directly proportional to the applied force.

On Higher tier papers you may have to choose the scales for the axes. You should make sure your graph covers over half of the grid.

On page 14 you saw some results for the volume of a gas under different pressures. Here they are again.

pressure in kPa	100	140	195	275	330	500
volume in cm^3	25	18	13	9	7.5	5

GCSE Mathematics for Scientists

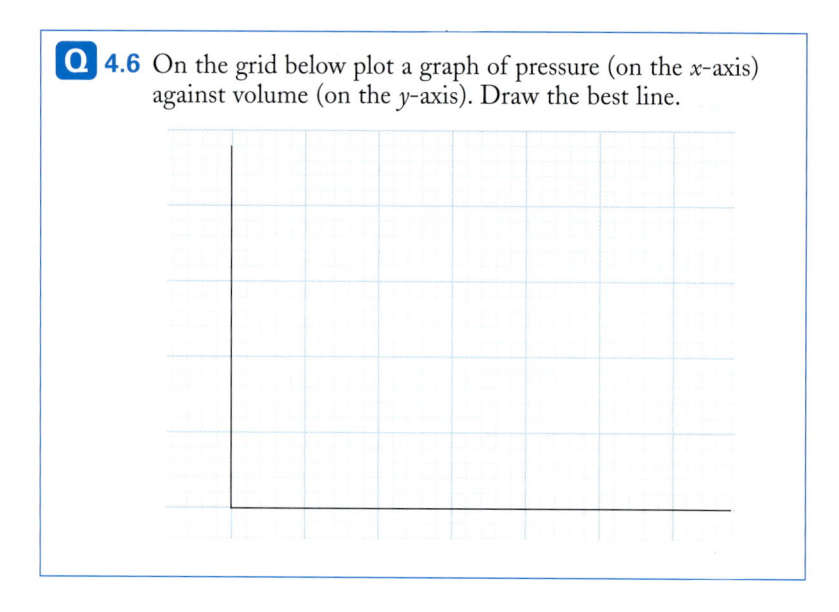

Q 4.6 On the grid below plot a graph of pressure (on the *x*-axis) against volume (on the *y*-axis). Draw the best line.

Q 4.7 a Now work out the **reciprocal** of volume, i.e. $\frac{1}{V}$. Correct your answer to three decimal places.

pressure in kPa	100	140	195	275	330	500
volume in cm³	25	18	13	9	7.5	5
$\frac{1}{V}$ in per cm³						

Plot these results on the grid in question 4.6. Draw the best line.

b What can you conclude from this graph?

It is more difficult to draw a curve than a straight line. To start with, make sure your pencil is sharp. Draw a smooth curve but do not worry if the curve does not go through all of the points.

4 Handling data

This diagram shows two graphs on the same grid. The graph labelled L is for large marble chips and S is for the same mass of small chips.

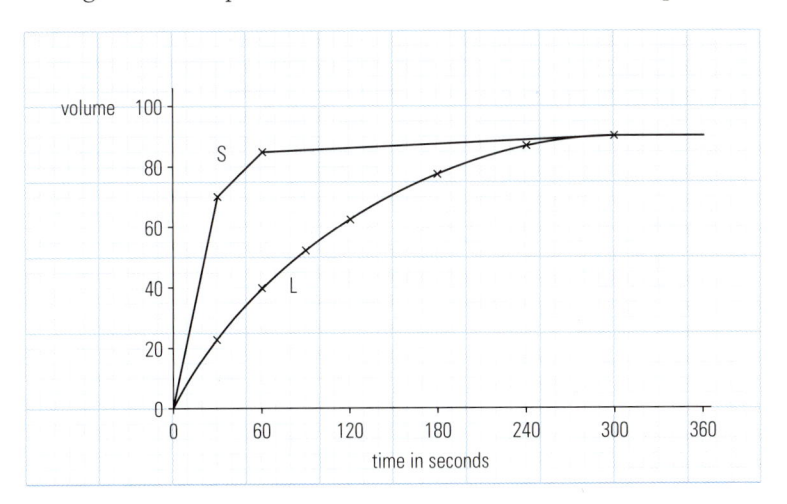

The same volume of acid is used at the same concentration and at the same temperature. Only the surface area of the marble chips is altered. The curve for L is good but the curve for S is not and would not score a mark. The curve is not smooth.

On Higher tier papers you may be given one or more anomalous results. When you look at the results you have plotted, anomalous results should be obviously off any line you could draw. You must ignore anomalous results when you plot a line of best fit.

> **Q 4.8** Here is a set of results for medium-sized marble chips. Plot these results on the previous grid and draw the **line of best fit** ignoring any anomalous results.
>
> | time in seconds | 0 | 30 | 60 | 90 | 120 | 150 | 180 | 210 | 240 |
> |---|---|---|---|---|---|---|---|---|---|
> | volume of gas collected in cm^3 | 0 | 34 | 58 | 66 | 74 | 78 | 84 | 87 | 90 |

Remember, each time you make a plot there is some uncertainty about the result. You could perhaps draw a circle around each plot and be sure that the actual result should be somewhere in that circle. The more inaccurate the experiment, the larger is the circle. You can be sure that any curve you draw should go through every circle even if it does not go through every point.

GCSE Mathematics for Scientists

Getting information from a graph

When you draw a graph in an experiment or on an examination paper, it is usually used to obtain information.

If you go back to the graph on page 36, you can find the volume of the gas when a pressure of 300 kPa is applied. Find 300 kPa on the x-axis. Put your ruler vertically at this point and make a mark on the curve. Where your ruler crosses the line, read off the volume. You should get an answer of 8.2 cm^3.

> **Q 4.9 a** Now find the volume of the gas when the pressure is 160 kPa.
>
> _____ cm^3.
>
> **b** What is the applied pressure when the volume is 20 cm^3?
>
> _____ kPa

A graph can also be used to see a pattern in results.

The results in this table are for the velocity of an object over a period of 30 seconds. The object is stationary at the start.

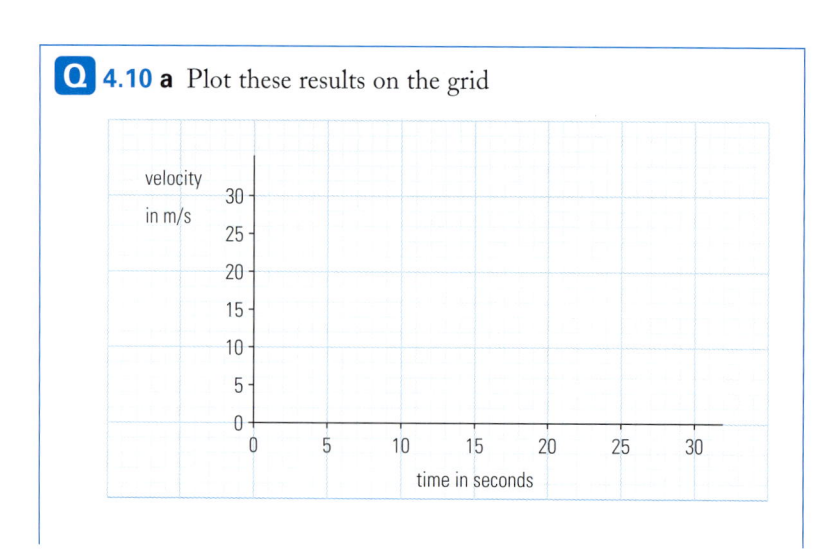

time in seconds	0	5	10	15	20	25	30
velocity in m/s	0	7	14	21	28	28	28

> **Q 4.10 a** Plot these results on the grid

b What is the maximum velocity of the object?

_____ m/s

c How long does it take the object to reach this maximum velocity?

_____ s

d How do you know the acceleration is constant?

_____

_____

We can find out the acceleration of the object by finding the **gradient** or steepness of the graph.

This diagram shows how the gradient can be found by drawing the largest possible right-angled triangle, working out the values for the velocity and time from the y and x axes and then dividing y by x.

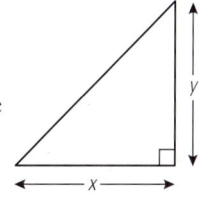

gradient = $\frac{y}{x}$

The distance travelled by the object in the first 20 seconds can be found by multiplying the average velocity (the velocity after 10 seconds) by time.

Distance travelled = 14 × 20 = 280 m

Alternatively, it can be found from the area under the graph up to 20 seconds. This is a triangle, and the area of the triangle can be found from

$$\text{area} = 0.5 \times \text{height of triangle} \times \text{base of triangle}$$
$$\text{distance travelled} = 0.5 \times 28 \times 20$$
$$= 280 \text{ m}$$

GCSE Mathematics for Scientists

Q 4.11 This diagram shows a graph of the velocity of another object over a period of 30 seconds.

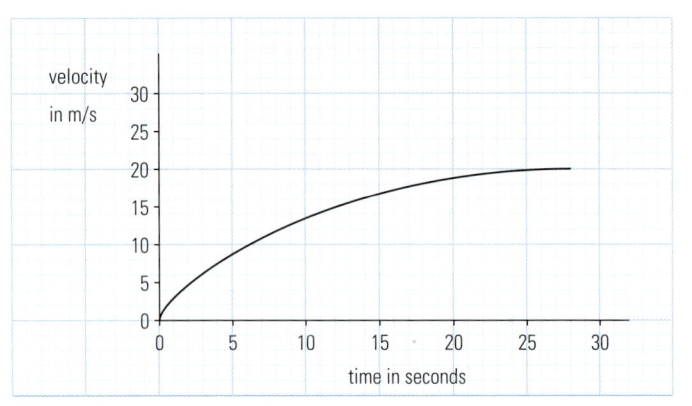

velocity in m/s vs *time in seconds*

a After how many seconds is the velocity 10 m/s?

_____

b Calculate the acceleration after 5 s. You have to draw a large right-angled triangle whose longest side is a tangent to the curve at 5 s (see page 39). Then work out the gradient of the longest side.

c Work out the distance travelled in 30 s. (Look back to page 25 to remind you how to find the area of an irregular shape.)

Q 4.12 On page 30 there are results for a rate of reaction experiment. Use the blank sheet of graph paper at the back of this booklet. Draw graphs of time (on y axis) against concentration (on x axis), and rate (on y axis) against concentration on the x axis.

4 Handling data

Statistical terms

This histogram shows the heights of a group of people. If you are asked to work out the average height, this can lead to some confusion as the word **average** can have different meanings. It is better to use the words **mode**, **median** and **mean**.

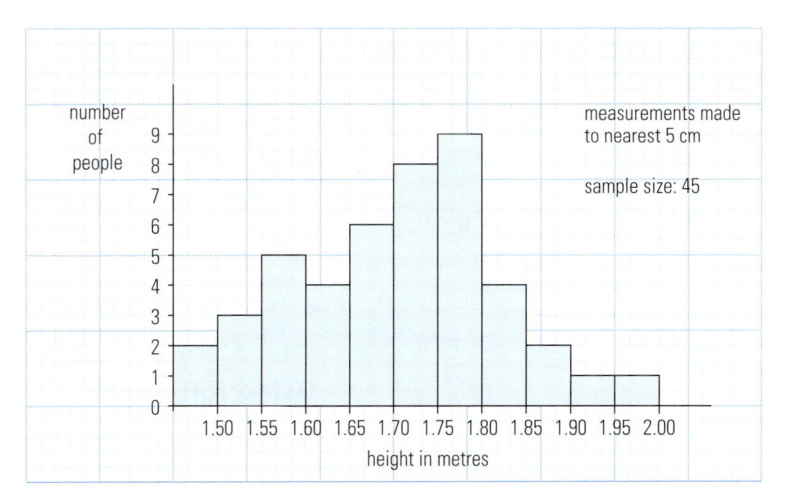

[Histogram: number of people (y-axis, 0–9) vs height in metres (x-axis, 1.50–2.00). Measurements made to nearest 5 cm. Sample size: 45.]

- The **mode** is the value which appears most often. In the example, it is 1.7 m.
- If the values are put in increasing order, the middle value is called the **median**. In this example, it is 1.75 m.
- The **mean** (m) is calculated by adding together all the values (x) and dividing by the total number (n):

$$m = \frac{\Sigma x}{n}$$

where Σ stands for 'the sum of'.

Q 4.13 The number of flowers on different plants were found. Six plants were found to have 5 flowers, 3 plants had four flowers, 7 plants had three flowers, 4 plants had two flowers, 2 plants had one flower and 1 plant had no flowers.

Calculate the **mean** of number of flowers on each plant.

Answers

Using a calculator

Q 1.1
a 10.3 **b** 101 **c** 23.5
d 24.1 **e** 12.0

Q 1.2
a ii **b** ii **c** ii **d** ii

Q 1.3
a **i** 295 **ii** 161.85 **iii** 501
   iv 449.837 **v** 1662.45
b **i** 350 − 273 = 77 **ii** 117.2
   iii 10.21 **iv** 112.7 **v** 215.27
c **i** 221 **ii** 59.77 **iii** 18.848
   iv 0.0675 **v** 101775
d **i** 8 **ii** 9.2 **iii** 5.64
   iv 11.18 **v** 4.82

Q 1.4
a 121 **b** 10000 **c** 174.24
d 0.0144 **e** 1.04

Q 1.5
a **i** 11 **ii** 9 **iii** 6
   iv 12 **v** 300
b **i** 14.14 **ii** 21.35 **iii** 4.84
   iv 1.86 **v** 0.077

Q 1.6
Numerator 3 Denominator 4

Q 1.7

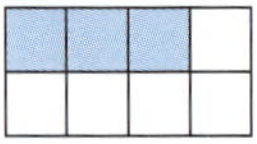

Any three squares shaded. $\frac{5}{8}$

Q 1.8
a $\frac{20}{40}$ $\frac{24}{48}$ **b** $\frac{9}{15}$ $\frac{15}{25}$ $\frac{6}{10}$ $\frac{12}{20}$

Q 1.9
a Four tenths.
b One tenth and two hundredths, or 12 hundredths
c Three tenths, seven hundredths and five thousandths, or 375 thousandths
d One unit, two tenths and five thousandths, or one and two hundred and five thousandths.
e Six units and seven thousandths.

Q 1.10
a **i** 0.25 **ii** 0.33 **iii** 0.875
   iv 0.6 **e** 0.364
b **i** $\frac{3}{4}$ **ii** $\frac{9}{20}$ **iii** $\frac{27}{40}$
   iv $\frac{19}{20}$ **v** $\frac{6}{25}$

Q 1.11
a **i** 50% **ii** 75% **iii** 62.5%
   iv 54.5% **v** 92.5%
b **i** $\frac{4}{5}$ **ii** $\frac{3}{25}$ **iii** $\frac{9}{20}$
   iv $\frac{93}{100}$ **v** $\frac{13}{20}$
c Percentage of oxygen =
   100 − (52.2 + 13.0) = 34.8%

Using formulae

Q 2.1
$$\text{Pressure} = \frac{\text{Force}}{\text{Area}} = \frac{100\,\text{N}}{20\,\text{cm}^2} = 5\,\text{N/cm}^2$$

or $\dfrac{100\,\text{N}}{0.002\,\text{m}^2} = 5000\,\text{N/m}^2$

Q 2.2
a Work = force × distance travelled
50 J = 10 N × distance in m
distance in m = $\frac{50}{10}$ = 5 m
or $W = Fd$
$d = \frac{W}{F} = \frac{50}{10} = 5\,\text{m}$
or
$d = \frac{W}{F} = \frac{50}{10} = 5\,\text{m}$

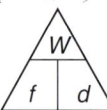

b Wave speed = frequency × wavelength $v = f\lambda$
1500 m/s = 250 Hz × λ
$\lambda = \dfrac{1500}{250} = 6\,\text{m}$

or

$v = f\lambda \quad \lambda = \dfrac{v}{f} = \dfrac{1500}{250} = 6\,\text{m}$

or

$\lambda = \dfrac{v}{f} \quad \dfrac{1500}{250} = 6\,\text{m}$

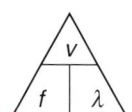

Answers

c   Pressure = $\frac{\text{Force}}{\text{Area}}$ = $\frac{100\,000\,\text{Pa}}{6\,\text{m}^2}$ = Force in N

Force = 600 000 N

or $P = \frac{F}{A}$

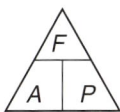

$F = AP$
= 6 × 100 000 N
= 600 000 N

Q 2.3
a   Work done lifting car = force × distance travelled = 800 × 10 × 1.8 = 14 440 J

b   Speed = $\frac{\text{distance}}{\text{time}}$,

so time taken = $\frac{\text{distance}}{\text{speed}}$ = $\frac{1.8}{0.2}$ = 9 s

Power = $\frac{\text{work done}}{\text{time taken}}$ = $\frac{14\,400}{9}$ = 1600 W

Q 2.4

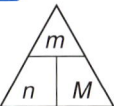

Q 2.5
a   1 mol of K_2O = 39 + 39 + 16 = 94 g
    9.4 g = 0.1 mol
b   1 mol of KOH = 39 + 16 + 1 = 56 g
    0.2 mol KOH = 11.2 g
c   1 mol of H_2O = 16 + 1 + 1 = 18 g
    0.5 mol H_2O = 9 g
d   0.1 mol KOH dissolved in 100 g of water is equivalent to 1 mol KOH dissolved in 1 dm^3 of water. Answer 56 g

Measuring length, mass and time

Q 3.1
Kilometres   km

Q 3.2
a   i   27.4 cm   ii   0.9 cm   iii   132 cm
b   i   1490 mm   ii   1450 mm   iii   127 mm
c   i   32 mm   ii   3.2 cm
d   i   50 mm 5 cm
    ii 43 mm 4.3 cm
    iii 61 mm 6.1 cm

Q 3.3
b, d and e

Q 3.4
a   i   105 s   ii   187 s   iii   323 s
b   i   3 min 0 s   ii   1 min 6 s
    iii 2 min 24 s

Q 3.5
a   10.1 s   b   12.5 s   c   11.1 s

Q 3.6
29 + 11 = 40 cm^2

Q 3.7
1000 dm^3

Q 3.8
a   7.0 cm

b $\frac{7.8}{3}$ = 2.6 cm

c   It makes the mayfly nymph appear larger than the stonefly nymph, although it is in fact smaller.

Q 3.9
a   Perimeter = 10 + 4 + 10 + 4 = 28 cm
b   12 and 1   1 and 2   10 and 3
    9 and 4   8 and 5   7 and 6

Q 3.10

length in cm	breadth in cm	area in cm^2
6	4	**24**
7	5	**35**
12	2	24
12.3	1.9	**23.4**
13	**7.15**	93

Q 3.11
a   125 cm^3 b   10 cm
c   9.5 cm × 6 cm = 57 cm^2 $\frac{1000}{57}$ = 17.5

Handling data

Q 4.1

| sector of leaf | number of aphids | |
	in wind	after wind
1	7	5
2	10	7
3	9	6
4	14	7
5	7	8
6	4	4
total	51	37

43

GCSE Mathematics for Scientists

Q 4.2
a 10%
b (pie chart showing: others, oil, solid fuel, gas)

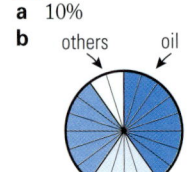

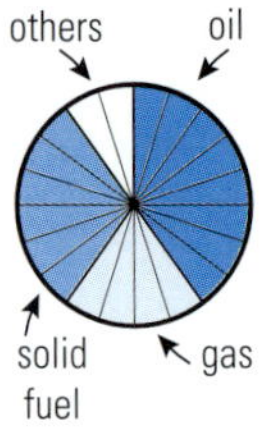

Q 4.3
Zinc 28 years   Copper 45 years
Iron 196 years   Aluminium 258 years
It is impossible to be exact from these diagrams.

Q 4.4
Southampton 210 mg/dm^3

Q 4.5
(graph: extension in mm vs force in N, straight line through origin)

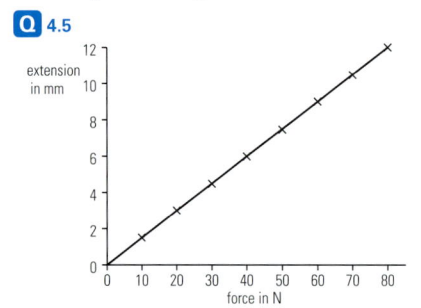

Q 4.6
(graph: volume in cm^3 vs pressure in kPa, inverse curve)

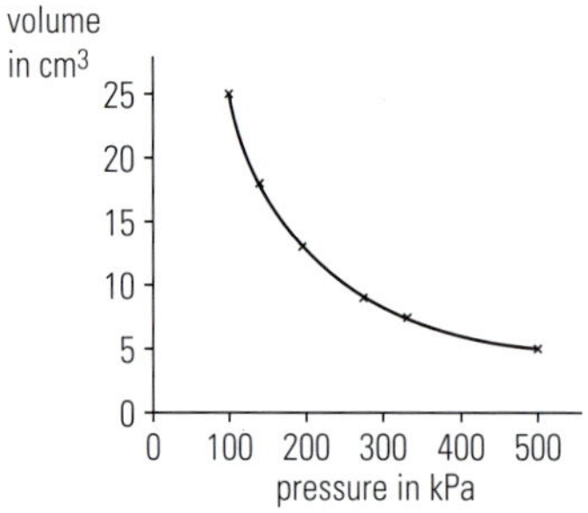

Q 4.7
a 0.040 0.056 0.077 0.111 0.133 0.200
b Pressure is directly proportional to $\frac{1}{V}$
   (The graph is a straight line)

Q 4.8
(graph: volume vs time in seconds, curves S, M, L)

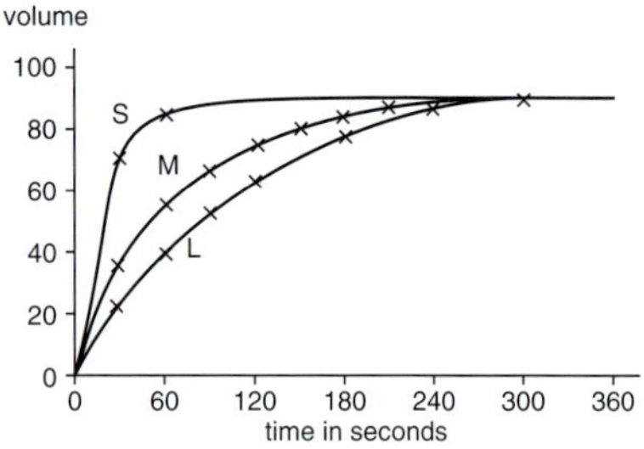

Q 4.9
a 16 cm^3
b 125 kPa

Q 4.10
a (velocity-time graph)

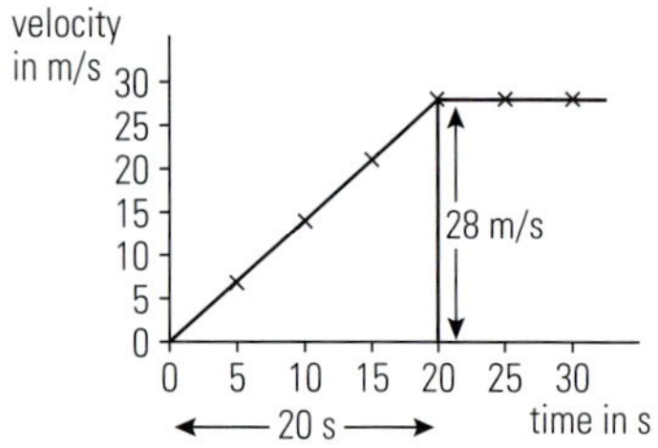

Acceleration = $\frac{28}{20}$
             = 1.4 m/s^2

b 28 m/s
c 20 s
d The graph is a straight line.

Q 4.11
a 6 s
b acceleration = $\frac{24}{20}$ = 1.2 m/s^2 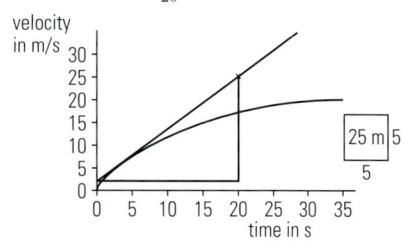
   (velocity-time graph, 25 m / 5)
c Distance travelled = area under the graph.
   Approximately 525 m (21 squares each 5 m/s by 5 s)
   N.B. This answer can only be approximate

Q 4.12

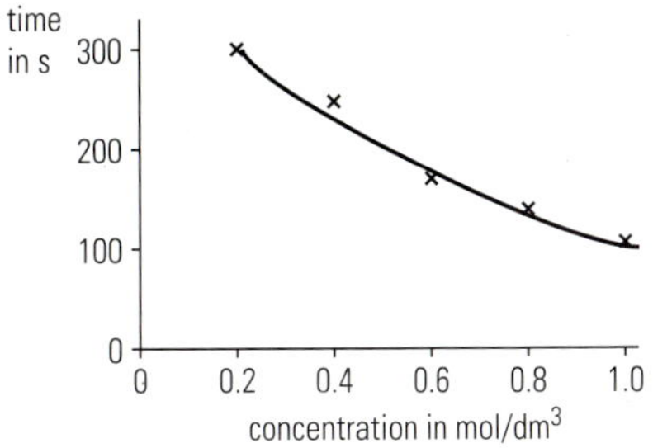
time
in s
300
200
100
0
0
0.2
0.4
0.6
0.8
1.0
concentration in mol/dm3

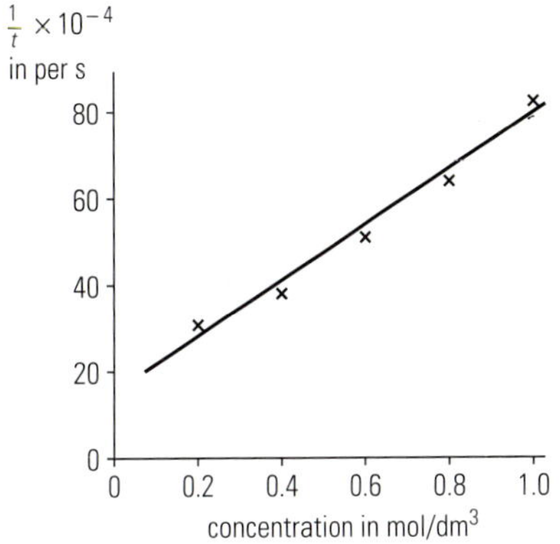
1/t × 10−4
in per s
80
60
40
20
0
0
0.2
0.4
0.6
0.8
1.0
concentration in mol/dm3

Q 4.13

Mean =

$$\frac{(6 \times 5) + (3 \times 4) + (7 \times 3) + (4 \times 2) + (2 \times 1) + (1 \times 0)}{6 + 3 + 7 + 4 + 2 + 1}$$

$= \frac{73}{23} = 3.2$